BREAKING THE CODE REVISED EDITION
UNDERSTANDING THE BOOK OF REVELATION
LEADER GUIDE

BREAKING THE CODE REVISED EDITION: UNDERSTANDING THE BOOK OF REVELATION

Breaking the Code Revised Edition

978-1-5018-8150-3
978-1-5018-8151-0 *eBook*

Breaking the Code: DVD

978-1-5018-8154-1

Breaking the Code: Leader Guide

978-1-5018-8152-7
978-1-5018-8153-4 *eBook*

For more information, visit www.abingdonpress.com.

BRUCE M. METZGER

REVISED AND UPDATED BY DAVID A. DESILVA

BREAKING THE CODE

UNDERSTANDING THE BOOK OF
REVELATION

LEADER GUIDE

by Barbara Dick

Abingdon Press/Nashville

BREAKING THE CODE REVISED EDITION
Understanding the Book of Revelation
Leader Guide

ISBN 978-1-5018-8152-7

19 20 21 22 23 24 25 26 27 28 — 10 9 8 7 6 5 4 3 2 1
MANUFACTURED IN THE UNITED STATES OF AMERICA

CONTENTS

TO THE LEADER

Welcome! In this study, you have the opportunity to help a group of learners explore the Book of Revelation through the eyes of an outstanding scholar and to begin to understand the book's impact on our life of faith.

Revelation has been a difficult book for many people to read. The meaning of its symbolism has been debated for centuries. Some of the dramatic scenes of violence may make group members uncomfortable. Consider how to create the kind of learning environment in which participants can share their understanding and feelings honestly, listen to others with sensitivity, and explore the book's richness alongside one another.

Scripture tells us that where two or three are gathered together, we can be assured of the presence of the Holy Spirit, working in and through all those gathered. As you prepare to lead, pray for that presence and expect that you will experience it.

This six-session study makes use of the following components:

- the study book, *Breaking the Code: Understanding the Book of Revelation* by Bruce M. Metzger, updated and revised by David A. deSilva;
- this Leader Guide;
- the *Breaking the Code* DVD.

Participants in the study will also need Bibles, as well as either a spiral-bound notebook for a journal or an electronic means of journaling, such as a tablet. If possible, notify those interested in the study in advance of the first session. Make arrangements for them to get copies of the study book so that they can read the prefaces and chapters 1–2.

USING THIS GUIDE WITH YOUR GROUP

Because no two groups are alike, this guide has been designed to give you flexibility and choice in tailoring the sessions for your group. The session format is listed below. You may choose any or all of the activities, adapting them as you wish to meet the schedule and needs of your particular group. As you make your selections, keep in mind the experience and knowledge level of your group. Beginning Bible study groups will need more guidance on finding and interpreting Scripture passages and references. Advanced Bible study groups may want to add outside study to the sessions.

Most sessions' available time will be too short to do all the activities. Select ahead of time which activities the group will do, for how long, and in what order. In some sessions, media and other multisensory aids are suggested in addition to the session videos. While these resources can enhance the group experience, they are not essential to the study. Depending on which activities you select, there may be special preparation needed; this preparation will be noted at the beginning of the session plan.

SESSION FORMAT

The Book of Revelation is complex, and the imagery and subject matter can be overwhelming; therefore, the sessions in this Leader Guide follow a simple format that repeats each session. Below is an outline of the session content, followed by more details of key items.

Planning the Session
- Session Goals
  - » *Understand* biblical terminology
  - » *Reflect* on the assigned passages
  - » *Explore* new ideas
  - » *Assess* personal and community discipleship
- Key Verse(s)
- Special Preparation

Getting Started
- Welcome
- Opening Prayer
- Opening Activities

Learning Together
- Video Study and Discussion
- Sources and Comparisons
- Breaking the Code
- Practical Revelations
- Closing Prayer

Next Session

Planning the Session includes foundational information of *Session Goals* and *Key Verse(s)* and *Special Preparation*, which instructs the leader on materials and setting up.

Getting Started offers an *Opening Prayer* (or you may use a prayer of your own) and *Opening Activities*, which seek to link the previous session to the current one.

9

Learning Together will follow a similar format each session: *Video Study and Discussion* invites response to the related *Breaking the Code* video (DVD available) and the session's main ideas; *Sources and Comparisons* explores Old Testament and other sources for the related material in Revelation; *Breaking the Code* includes exercises and activities focused on the related material in Revelation itself; *Practical Revelations* invites the group to explore the practical applications and implications for discipleship provided by the Book of Revelation; *Closing Prayer* is offered in each session (or you may use a prayer of your own).

Next Session in Sessions 1–5 gives suggestions for group members' preparation for their next gathering. This list will include readings from *Breaking the Code* and the Book of Revelation and topics for journaling and reflecting.

As mentioned already, there are more activities and discussions for each session than most groups will be able to get through. Plan ahead of time which ones you will explore in each session based on your group's interests, learning styles, and other characteristics.

HELPFUL HINTS

Preparing for the Session

- Pray for the leading of the Holy Spirit as you prepare for the study. Pray for discernment for yourself and for each member of the study group.
- Before each session, familiarize yourself with the content. Read again the book chapters and related chapters of Revelation.
- Choose the session elements you will use during the group session, including the specific discussion questions you plan to cover. Be prepared, however, to adjust the session as group members interact and as questions arise. Prepare carefully, but

allow space for the Holy Spirit to move in and through group members and through you as facilitator.

- Obtain appropriate projection equipment for video and media, and test it before the session in which you plan to use it.
- Prepare the space where the group will meet so that the space will enhance the learning process. Ideally, group members should be seated around a table or in a circle so that all can see one another. Movable chairs are best, because the group will often form pairs or small groups for discussion.
- Bring a supply of Bibles for those who forget to bring their own. Provide a variety of translations.
- For most sessions you will also need an easel with paper and markers, a markerboard and markers, or some other means of posting group questions and responses.

Shaping the Learning Environment

- Establish a welcoming space. Consider the room temperature, access to amenities, hospitality, outside noise, and privacy. Use a small cross or candle as a focal point for times of prayer.
- Create a climate of openness, encouraging group members to participate as they feel comfortable. As mentioned above, some participants may be uncomfortable with some of the subject matter. Be on the lookout for signs of discomfort in those who may be silent, and encourage them to express their thoughts and feelings honestly, but assure the group members that passing on a question is always acceptable.
- Some people will jump right in with answers and comments, while others need time to process what is being discussed. If you notice that some group members seem never to be able to enter the conversation, ask them if they have thoughts to share. Give everyone a chance to talk, but keep the conversation moving. Moderate to prevent a few individuals from doing all the talking.

11

- Make use of the exercises that invite sharing in pairs. Those who are reluctant to speak out in a group setting may be more comfortable sharing one-on-one and reporting back to the group. This can often be an effective means of helping people grow more comfortable sharing in the larger setting. It also helps to avoid the dominance of the group by one or two participants (including you!).
- If no one answers at first during discussions, do not be afraid of silence. Help the group become comfortable with waiting. If no one responds, try reframing the language of the question. If no responses are forthcoming, venture an answer yourself and ask for comments.
- Model openness as you share with the group. Group members will follow your example. If you limit your sharing to a surface level, others will follow suit.
- Encourage multiple answers or responses before moving on.
- Ask, "Why?" or "Why do you believe that?" or "Can you say more about that?" to help continue a discussion and give it greater depth.
- Affirm others' responses with comments such as "Great" or "Thanks" or "Good insight"—especially if it's the first time someone has spoken during the group session.
- Monitor your own contributions. If you are doing most of the talking, back off so that you do not train the group to listen rather than speak up.
- Remember that you do not have all the answers. Your job is to keep the discussion going and encourage participation.

Managing the Session

- Begin and end on time.
- Honor the time schedule. If a session is running longer than expected, get consensus from the group before continuing beyond the agreed-upon ending time.

- When someone arrives late or *must* leave early, pause the session *briefly* to welcome them or bid them farewell. Change in the makeup of the group changes the dynamics of the discussion and needs to be acknowledged. Every group member is important to the entire group.
- Involve group members in various aspects of the group session, such as saying prayers or reading Scripture.
- As always in discussions that may involve personal sharing, confidentiality is essential. Group members should never pass along stories that have been shared in the group. Remind group members at each session: honoring confidentiality is crucial to the success of this study.

Session 1
INTRODUCTION AND JOHN'S VISION

Covering the following chapters from the study book:

Chapter 1: Introducing the Book of Revelation
Chapter 2: John's Vision of the Heavenly Christ
Revelation 1:1-20

PLANNING THE SESSION

Session Goals

As a result of conversations and activities connected with this session, group members should begin to

- understand the meaning of *apocalypse* and *disciplined imagination*;
- reflect on apocalyptic Bible passages;
- explore the use of symbolism in Revelation;
- assess their comfort with the style of writing in Revelation.

Key Verse

*Blessed is the one who reads aloud the words of the prophecy,
and blessed are those who hear and who keep what is written
in it; for the time is near.*

(Revelation 1:3)

Special Preparation

- If possible in advance of the first session, ask participants to bring either a spiral-bound notebook or an electronic means of journaling, such as a tablet. Provide writing paper and pens for those who may need them. Also have a variety of Bibles available for those who do not bring one.
- Make sure all participants have a copy of the study book, *Breaking the Code*. Invite them to read the prefaces and chapters 1–2 in advance of the first session. You also should read this material.
- If group members are not familiar with one another, make nametags available.
- Have available a markerboard, large sheets of blank paper, or construction paper and colored markers.
- At the top of two columns, on markerboard or large paper, place the words *Alpha* and *Omega*.

Remember that there are more activities than most groups will have time to complete. As leader, you'll want to go over the session in advance and select or adapt the activities you think will work best for your group in the time allotted. Consider your own responses to questions you will pose to the group.

GETTING STARTED

Welcome

As participants arrive, welcome them to the study and invite them to make use of one of the available Bibles, if they did not bring one.

15

Opening Prayer

Gracious and loving God, as we begin this study, open us to your presence and fill us—our time, our conversations, our reflections, our doubts, and our fears—with the joy of exploration and the wisdom of your love. We gather together in Jesus' name. Amen.

Opening Activities

When all participants have arrived, invite each person to introduce himself or herself by name and to offer a definition or response to the posted words (*Alpha*; *Omega*). Record responses in the appropriate columns. Assure participants that these responses provide only a starting place for the study. New understandings will emerge during the study sessions.

If they have not already done read it, invite group members to silently and briefly skim chapter 1 in the study book. Explore together:

- In the preface to the revised edition (p. 11), David A. deSilva declares:

  > While individual study will always be rewarding, Revelation is a text that is perhaps best heard and studied in community. It was written and first read to gathered assemblies in the context of worship and prayer; its word was conceived of as "what the Spirit is saying to the churches," and not to lone disciples. Its challenge is most fully and readily met by groups of disciples working together to discover and embody its word, and its ultimate goal is to call into being a new way of being human together before God.

- Invite participants to share responses to this statement. Share that calling "into being a new way of being human together before God" will be the ultimate goal of this study.

- Bruce M. Metzger, the author, identifies four types of biblical literature: that which touches our *emotions*, speaks to our *will*, appeals to our *intellect*, and sparks our *imagination*. Invite participants to locate samples of each type of biblical literature (they may use the samples given in the introduction). Ask if they agree or disagree with the author's characterizations of biblical literature, and why or why not.
- The author further defines the appeal of Revelation as to *disciplined imagination*. Invite participants to share their understanding of that phrase and why they believe the author adds the element of discipline.

LEARNING TOGETHER

Video Study and Discussion

The Session 1 video explores the nature of John's vision and the Book of Revelation. Play the Session 1 video, titled "John's Vision," and explore together the following questions:

- What is one thing you learned in the video that you did not know before?
- How does it change your impression of Revelation to know that the word *apocalypse* means "unveiling," not "disaster"?
- What do you expect this study of Revelation to "unveil" to you?
- David deSilva remarks that "John sees as the Scriptures have given him eyes to see." How has Scripture opened your eyes to see things differently? How do you expect Revelation to open your eyes in a new way?
- What does John seem to be revealing in his vision about Christ, about his reign, and about the urgency of living rightly in our world?

Sources and Comparisons

Apocalypse

Revelation is written in the literary style of *apocalypse* (disclosure or unveiling). John draws heavily on images and symbols from Hebrew Scriptures. We will explore several aspects of this literature from our Old Testament throughout our study. We begin here with just a few examples of biblical texts that include "dreams, visions, and conversations . . . with . . . superhuman figures" (p. 23). Form four small groups or pairs and assign one of the texts listed below to each group. Ask them to identify what the writer sees and hears. When the groups have had time to work, ask them to share with the larger group. Make note of common features among the passages (keep these for reference in Session 3).

- Isaiah 6:1-13
- Ezekiel 1–2
- Daniel 7:1-14
- Revelation 1:9-20

Ask participants if the passages were clear or confusing, upsetting or inspiring, or produced some other response. Let them know that one of the goals of this study will be to bring both clarity and inspiration to their understanding of Revelation and apocalyptic literature.

Breaking the Code

Who? When? Where? What? Why?

Divide the group into pairs. Invite each pair to answer the listed questions, using chapters 1–2 and the maps on page 26 as source material:

- Who is John?
- When was Revelation written?

- Where is Patmos?
- Where are the seven churches?
- What is the stated goal for John sharing his visions?

When the pairs have had time to work, invite them to share their responses to the last question, the *why* of Revelation. Ask participants to share what they have learned about the first-century context of the book and why John felt such urgency in sharing it with the churches.

Symbolic Language

Invite a volunteer to read Revelation 1:12-16.

Lead a conversation on what participants see as the significance of John's repeated use of the number seven and other symbolic language.

In the section on the first vision, the author states that the description of the vision "does not mean what it says; it means what it means" (p. 34). Ask participants to share their understanding of that statement.

It may be helpful at this point to define the terms *metaphor* (a figure of speech that uses one kind of object or idea in place of another) and *simile* (a figure of speech that compares two ideas or objects to suggest the similarity between them). Verses 12-16 include a number of similes. Invite participants to identify them (for example, "eyes like a flame of fire," "feet like burnished bronze," "voice like the sound of many waters") and share why they believe John uses this type of language. How does the author of the study book help them understand the vision?

Practical Revelations

Imperialism vs. God's Kingdom

John's first-century audience was living under the oppression of Roman imperial rule, as well as the pressure to "fit in" by worshiping idols (including the "divine" emperor). John compares this with God's kingdom—Alpha and Omega—that was here before Rome came into being and that will be here long after Rome falls. God's kingdom, presented in symbolic, awe-inspiring language, will be fully realized when Christ returns in glory.

We have reflected on the urgency of John's message for its first hearers. Now invite participants to reflect in silence on the urgency of the message for our Christian discipleship today. Suggest that they write or draw an expression of that message for their own lives.

Beatitudes

The Bible verse chosen as foundation for this session is Revelation 1:3. The author identifies this as the first of seven *beatitudes* or blessings, scattered throughout the book (1:3; 14:13; 16:15; 19:9; 20:6; 22:7, 14). Provide them as a printed handout (with space below each one for notes) or invite participants to copy them into their notebooks or journals. Ask for volunteers to read the verses aloud.

- 1:3—"Blessed is the one who reads aloud the words of the prophecy, and blessed are those who hear and who keep what is written in it; for the time is near."
- 14:13—" 'Blessed are the dead who from now on die in the Lord.' 'Yes,' says the Spirit, 'they will rest from their labors, for their deeds follow them.' "
- 16:15—"('See, I am coming like a thief! Blessed is the one who stays awake and is clothed, not going about naked and exposed to shame.')"
- 19:9—" 'Blessed are those who are invited to the marriage supper of the Lamb.' And he said to me, 'These are true words of God.' "
- 20:6—"Blessed and holy are those who share in the first resurrection. Over these the second death has no power, but they will be priests of God and of Christ, and they will reign with him a thousand years."
- 22:7—"See, I am coming soon! Blessed is the one who keeps the words of the prophecy of this book."

- 22:14—"Blessed are those who wash their robes, so that they will have the right to the tree of life and may enter the city by the gates."

Share that one of the goals of this study is for participants to clearly understand the meaning and significance of these beatitudes for their individual lives, for the life of the group, and for the life of the church.

Closing Prayer

Alpha and Omega, everlasting God, fill us with your power as we leave this place, so that all we have shared and learned here helps us to be more faithful disciples. As your church in and for the world, we pray in the name of Jesus the Christ. Amen.

NEXT SESSION

Invite participants to

- read chapters 3–4 in the study book and Revelation 2:1–3:22 in advance of the next session;
- reflect on and journal about the beatitudes listed above. Ask them to consider one insight they might want to share with the group about the first beatitude, Revelation 1:3.

Session 2
LETTERS TO CHURCHES

Covering the following chapters from the study book:
Chapter 3: Prophetic Words to the Churches
Chapter 4: More Prophetic Words to Churches
Revelation 2:1–3:22

PLANNING THE SESSION

Session Goals

As a result of conversations and activities connected with this session, group members should begin to

- understand the meaning of *oracle, stephanos, apostasy (fornication), second death, white, door, amen* in the context of Revelation;
- reflect on biblical passages related to John's "letters" to the churches;

- explore the messages given to the churches and their significance in the ultimate goal of Revelation;
- assess what we have in common with the seven churches, in challenges and triumphs.

Key Verse

"Let anyone who has an ear listen to what the Spirit is saying to the churches."

(Revelation 3:22)

Special Preparation

- Ask participants to bring their notebooks or electronic journals. Provide writing paper and pens for those who may need them. Have a variety of Bibles available for those who do not bring one.
- Have available for viewing, either electronically or in print, Holman Hunt's painting *The Light of the World*. It can be seen at https://en.wikipedia.org/wiki/The_Light_of_the_World _(painting).
- Have available a markerboard, large sheets of blank paper or construction paper and colored markers.
- If group members are not familiar with one another, make nametags available.

Remember that there are more activities than most groups will have time to complete. As leader, you'll want to go over the session in advance and select or adapt the activities you think will work best for your group in the time allotted. Consider your own responses to questions you will pose to the group.

GETTING STARTED

Welcome

As participants arrive, welcome them to the study and invite them to make use of one of the available Bibles, if they did not bring one.

Opening Prayer

Calling God, we gather here to know you better, to learn ways for our lives to be more attuned to your will. Open us to your presence and assurance as we share our experiences and knowledge, our doubts and confusion. We humbly rely on you, Lord, and we pray in Jesus' name. Amen.

Opening Activities

When all participants have arrived, invite each person to introduce himself or herself by name and share which, if any, of the seven churches seems most familiar and why. Do not take notes during the introductions.

- Invite participants to share one new insight related to the first beatitude (Revelation 1:3) from their journals.
- Ask a volunteer to read aloud the first two paragraphs of chapter 3 of the study book. Invite participants to share responses to the author's suggestions regarding why the seven churches were chosen.
- The author characterizes the messages to the churches as *oracles* rather than *letters*. Invite participants to share whether or not they agree with the author and why.

LEARNING TOGETHER

Video Study and Discussion

The Session 2 video explores the letters to the churches in Revelation 2–3. Play the Session 2 video, titled "Letters to Churches," and explore together the following questions from the video:

- What do we need to keep in mind in order to follow Jesus faithfully in our setting?
- What in our lives, both individually and as a congregation, would meet with Jesus' approval?

- Where is our obedience to Jesus and our witness to his reign falling short?
- What promises from God do we need to take to heart?
- How can "the long view" of our lives and of the world, as revealed in Scripture, motivate better discipleship in the present moment?

Sources and Comparisons

These chapters focus on John's "letters" to the seven churches in Asia Minor. Divide into six pairs and assign each pair one of the cities for exploration (assign together Pergamum and Thyatira). If your group is too small for six pairs, assign the cities to individuals. Ask the pairs to locate the city on the map (p. 26), review the author's insights about the church there, find additional biblical references to the assigned city, and prepare a brief summary to share. If you have a good Wi-Fi connection, participants may want to look up the city and include historical information as well. The focus here is on the city itself, not on John's message to the church.

- Ephesus (Revelation 2:1-7)
- Smyrna (Revelation 2:8-11)
- Pergamum (Revelation 2:12-17)
- Thyatira (Revelation 2:18-29)
- Sardis (Revelation 3:1-6)
- Philadelphia (Revelation 3:7-13)
- Laodicea (Revelation 3:14-22)

When the pairs (or persons) have had time to work, invite them to share their summaries with the group.

Breaking the Code

Oracle Structure

Invite a volunteer to read the third paragraph from chapter 3 of the study book. Ask the same pairs to work together again and focus on assembling the oracle to their assigned churches following the author's pattern for the messages. If they believe an element is missing or does not follow the pattern, invite them to note that in their summary. Consider creating a handout chart with space for answers, based on the sample below.

- Christ identifies himself (What symbolic language is used?)
- Praise given for what the church has done/is doing well
- Statement of issues of concern
- Warnings of consequences for not hearing and heeding the *oracle*
- Promises for faithfulness and endurance

Church	Revelation Text	Christ Identified	Praises	Concerns	Warnings/ Consequences	Promises
Ephesus	2:1-7					
Smyrna	2:8-11					
Pergamum	2:12-17					
Thyatira	2:18-29					
Sardis	3:1-6					
Philadelphia	3:7-13					
Laodicea	3:14-22					

When the pairs have had time to work, invite them to share their answers with the group. If you have provided a handout chart, others in the group can fill in their charts as each pair shares what they have learned.

Making Meaning

The author introduces a variety of terms that will likely be unfamiliar to group members. It will be helpful to explore some of these that are foundational to the ultimate goal of Revelation: "to call into being a new way of being human together before God" (p. 11).

Form small groups to explore the terms and prepare definitions to share with the group. More than one term may be assigned to a group. Ask the groups to cite the location in the study book and/or Revelation that supports their definition.

- *stephanos* ("crown of life," 2:10)
- second death (2:11b)
- apostasy/fornication (2:21)
- conquer (2:7, 26; 3:5, 12, 21)
- white (stones [2:17], garments [3:4-5])
- door, standing at the door (make available the Holman Hunt painting referenced by the author) (3:8, 20)
- Christ as the Amen (3:14)

When the groups have had time to work, invite them to share their definitions and sources. Lead a conversation on the significance of each term to the ultimate goal of Revelation (see above).

Practical Revelations

Personal Discipleship

At the end of chapter 3, the author invites us to face the question: "How far should I accept and adopt contemporary standards and practices in business, social arrangements, and the like?" (p. 47). Invite participants to reflect on this question regarding their personal discipleship. When they have had time with the question, invite them to share responses with the person sitting next to them.

Community Discipleship

At the end of chapter 4, the author states:

> The message to each church is at the same time a message to all churches. The seven churches provide examples of the kinds of things that can go wrong

in any church. These are: the danger of losing the love that one had at first (Ephesus), fear of suffering (Smyrna), doctrinal compromise (Pergamum), moral compromise (Thyatira), spiritual deadness (Sardis), failure to hold fast (Philadelphia), and lukewarmness (Laodicea).

Invite participants to share ways that their faith communities may be struggling with any of these issues. As you identify the current struggles, share the author's understanding of the hope offered by Revelation: "They also provide direction and incentive to the churches of every nation and age to overcome—to *conquer*—these challenges to faithfulness and triumph together in the Lamb" (p. 58). Ask participants to share ways that they see their faith communities working to "conquer" challenges to faithfulness.

Closing Prayer

God of our failures and hopes, open our hearts to understand fully and share joyfully the lessons learned here about our own lives and the life of the community of faith. Help us to live our lives as reflections of your love and faithfulness, to rely on you as the source of our strength and our rest. As your church in and for the world, we pray in the name of Jesus the Christ. Amen.

NEXT SESSION

Invite participants to:

- read chapters 5–6 in the study book and Revelation 4:1–8:5 in advance of the next session;
- reflect on and journal about the beatitudes listed at the end of Session 1. Ask them to consider one insight they might want to share with the group about the third beatitude, Revelation 16:15.

Session 3
GOD, THE LAMB, AND SEVEN SEALS

Covering the following chapters from the study book:

Chapter 5: John's Vision of God and the Lamb
Chapter 6: Opening the Seven Seals of God's Scroll
Revelation 4:1–8:5

PLANNING THE SESSION

Session Goals

As a result of conversations and activities connected with this session, group members should begin to

- begin to understand the meaning of the *Lamb of God, Day of the Lord, free will*;
- reflect on biblical passages related to Christ as the Lamb of God;
- explore the meaning and symbolism of the seven seals;
- assess our discipleship in relation to free will and justice.

Key Verses

> "*To the one seated on the throne and to the Lamb*
> *be blessing and honor and glory and might*
> *forever and ever!*"
> (Revelation 5:13b)

> *I saw another angel ascending from the rising of the sun,*
> *having the seal of the living God, and he called with a loud*
> *voice to the four angels who had been given power to damage*
> *earth and sea, saying, "Do not damage the earth or the sea or*
> *the trees, until we have marked the servants of our God with*
> *a seal on their foreheads."*
> (Revelation 7:2-3)

Special Preparation

- Ask participants to bring their notebooks or electronic journals. Provide writing paper and pens for those who may need them. Have a variety of Bibles available for those who do not bring one.
- Have available a markerboard, large sheets of blank paper or construction paper and colored markers.
- Have available samples or images of jasper, carnelian, emerald, and sapphire.
- Have available samples or images of medieval diptychs related to Revelation or of the four horsemen of the Apocalypse.
- If group members are not familiar with one another, make nametags available.

Remember that there are more activities than most groups will have time to complete. As leader, you'll want to go over the session in advance and select or adapt the activities you think will work best for your group in the time allotted. Consider your own responses to questions you will pose to the group.

GETTING STARTED

Welcome

As participants arrive, welcome them to the study and invite them to make use of one of the available Bibles, if they did not bring one.

Opening Prayer

All powerful, loving God of justice, as we share our reflections and learning in this time and place, help us to remember that you are the source and goal of everything in our lives—material and spiritual. We pray that this time together leads us to more faithful witness in a world hungry for your Word. Amen.

Opening Activities

When all participants have arrived, invite each person to introduce himself or herself by name and share their understanding of the four horsemen of the Apocalypse. Do not take notes during the introductions.

- Invite participants to share from their journals one new insight on the third beatitude (Revelation 16:15) or other reading.
- Ask a volunteer to read the first two paragraphs of chapter 5 in the study book, where the author speaks of the shift of activity from earth to heaven and the increasing difficulty of understanding the symbols of Revelation. Ask participants if they experienced this increased difficulty and, if so, in what ways. Remind the group of the author's call to use "disciplined imagination" in reading Revelation.
- Invite participants to share similes or symbolic language that is repeated from earlier chapters of Revelation (for example, seven, conquer, white garments/horse, open door). List these on a markerboard or large paper to help form a language bridge from the earthly to heavenly scenes.

LEARNING TOGETHER

Video Study and Discussion

The Session 3 video explores the central role of worship in the Book of Revelation, and of the power of worship and liturgy in our lives to center us around that which is most important. Play the Session 3 video, titled "God, the Lamb, and Seven Seals," and explore together the following questions taken from the video:

- Do our lives revolve around the correct center—that is, God and God's throne? In what ways are our daily attitudes and practices consistent with a life that is centered on God?
- What claims our allegiance ahead of or alongside God? What tempts us to orbit around a different center?
- How do our times in worship put us in touch with God and Christ to whom all honor is due? How does our worship re-center us on God?
- How will we encounter God when God intervenes in the world to set things right?

Sources and Comparisons

The Throne of God

In Session 1, we looked briefly at some Old Testament sources for John's imagery of the throne of God and heavenly attendants (see "Apocalypse" under the "Sources and Comparisons" section). Here we revisit a few of those passages for deeper understanding of the symbolism of that imagery. Divide into small groups of no more than four. Assign each group one of the passages listed below. Ask them to describe or draw the heavenly court and to talk about how they feel about and understand the images. Encourage the use of a variety of Bible translations and versions.

- Ezekiel 1:4-21; 10:1-5
- Isaiah 6:1-4
- Daniel 7:9-10
- Revelation 4:2-11

When the groups have had time to work, invite a spokesperson from each group to present their description or drawing. Using the list of notes from Session 1, add new areas of commonality. Invite the group to share new understandings of the imagery (for example, gems, fire or lightning, creatures with multiple eyes and wings). What does the author say about why the biblical writers used such dramatic images for depicting the throne of God and the heavenly court?

Lamb of God

In our Session 2 study of the oracles to the seven churches, we looked at some symbolic language used to describe Christ. Some of these occur again to describe Christ in the heavenly realm, but a new description is added: Christ is the Lamb of God, the only one worthy to open and read the sealed scrolls. The Old Testament includes nearly 150 references to lambs; most of them relate to offerings or sacrifice, focusing on the purity and spotless nature of the animals. Ask for volunteers to read the listed passages as examples.

- Exodus 12:3-8
- Leviticus 23:19-20
- 1 Samuel 17:34-35
- Isaiah 11:1-10
- Isaiah 53:7

Invite participants to follow along as you read Revelation 5. Have them read in unison the songs in verses 9-10, 12, and 13. Lead a conversation on why John uses the imagery of a lamb for Christ and what it might have meant to the first hearers. Ask how it felt to "sing" together the heavenly songs of praise.

Punishment of the Wicked

In chapter 6 of the study book, the author again lifts up John's use of Hebrew Scripture imagery to describe the punishment of the wicked upon the breaking of the sixth seal. Form small groups and assign each group one of the listed passages. Ask them to investigate the context for the referenced verses (who was the audience for the text; why was it written, and so forth?).

- Haggai 2:6 (earthquake)
- Joel 2:31 (sun turned black and moon turned to blood)
- Isaiah 34:4 (stars fallen from heaven, sky rolled up like a scroll)
- Jeremiah 4:23-26 (earthly chaos)

When the groups have had time to work, invite a spokesperson from each group to share what they have learned about these prophetic inspirations for Revelation. Then read Revelation 6:12-17. Ask how knowing the Old Testament origin of these images helps us to understand John's message.

Breaking the Code

Numbers

Revelation is filled with symbolic numbers, which we will encounter again and again. The author offers valuable insights on the significance and meaning of these numbers. Invite the participants to locate the listed numbers in the Revelation texts for this session and in chapters 5 and 6 of the study book.

- seven as the number of perfection (bowls, lamps, seals, trumpets, and so on)
- four living creatures
- twenty-four elders
- 144,000 Israelites, marked for protection

When the participants have had time to work, invite them to share what they have learned about the use of numbers in Revelation: what they would have meant to the first hearers, and how they can be meaningful for us today.

Seven Seals and Four Horsemen, and Silence

In Revelation, the series of seven events repeats through seals, trumpets, and bowls. The author shares that a basic outline is followed each time: the first four events occur as a group, followed by the fifth and sixth events in a pair; an interlude of some kind then precedes the seventh event in the series. We will explore them in these groupings.

Revelation 6:1-8 (First Four Seals): As each of the first four seals of God's scroll is opened, one of the four living creatures announces the arrival of a horse and rider, known collectively as the four horsemen of the Apocalypse. Ask participants if they are familiar with that term and in what contexts (movies, books, artwork). Note that this enlarges on the opening activity for this session.

Divide into four groups and assign one of the horsemen to each group. Invite them to explore the related colors, weapons, and actions, from Revelation 6:1-8 and the related sections of chapter 6 in the study book. If a group wishes, they may create a drawing of the horse and rider to share:

Horse color	Rider weapon, gifts	Assignment
White	Bow, crown	Conquer
Red	Great sword	Take peace, destroy, shatter
Black	Scales	Huge costs for food and the famine that results
Pale Green	Death with Hades	Sword, famine, pestilence, and death

When the groups have had time to work, invite them to share their findings and how they may differ from their previous experience with the four horsemen of the Apocalypse. Lead a conversation on the violence of the imagery (which we will revisit in later sessions). What was John trying to say to the churches by the use of such dramatic images?

Revelation 6:9-17 (Seals Five and Six): At the opening of the fifth seal, the souls of the martyrs are given comfort and told to be patient. Ask participants to share their understanding of the word *martyr*. What does the author tell us about them? (In the study book, in addition to the material in chapter 6, see also the sections "Time of Writing of Revelation" in chapter 1 and "The Oracle to the Church in Smyrna" in chapter 3.) Why does John draw our attention to them at this point in the vision?

If you did the exercise "Punishment of the Wicked" under "Sources and Comparisons" above, refer back to your notes. If not, consider the Old Testament comparisons listed there and lead a conversation on the question from verse 17: "Who is able to stand" on the great day of God's wrath? This offers opportunity to introduce the idea of the Day of the Lord (which we will revisit) and to offer space for participants to share their discomfort with the idea of a wrathful God. Look particularly at the author's approach to this idea, that the Day of the Lord is an inevitable outcome of an impenitent world, not willful destruction by a God who glories in punishment.

Revelation 7:1-17 (Protection of the 144,000): Participants will already have explored the number 144,000. Invite them to share their understanding of the reason the 144,000 and the great multitude are protected. Ask: Why John introduces this respite from wrath?

Revelation 8:1-5 (Seventh Seal and Silence): Ask participants why they believe there was silence at the opening of the seventh seal. What is significant about the opening of the final seal being accompanied by prayer (verses 4-5)?

Practical Revelations

Free Will

The author states that the Book of Revelation differs from other books in the New Testament in its attempt to "show how power fits into the divine scheme of things" (p. 72). God has given us free will, which also gives us the potential to misuse this power: "Ignore physical laws, like stepping off a cliff, and disaster follows. Neglect moral laws, and disaster ensues just as surely" (p. 73).

Ask the following questions:

- What does it mean to have free will if all power comes from God?
- What is the difference between God's righteousness and human power?
- How does that influence our relationship with God?

Remind the group that the idea of free will raises all sorts of tough questions that people have wrestled with for centuries. We can only scratch the surface of these questions right now, but if someone would like to learn more, invite them to do research and report back to the group next week. You might suggest that they start with the writings of Saint Augustine and John Wesley, which can be found online at www.ccel.org.

The Day of the Lord

"Who is able to stand" (6:17) on the Day of the Lord? This is the ultimate question in Revelation. As we will see again and again, the book draws stark contrast between those who have been faithful and those who have not. Is this an accurate depiction of humanity? Does it seem fair or just? Why or why not? In the author's words, "How do you wish to encounter God and the Lamb on that great Day? How does your answer...illumine the choices and challenges you must face today" (p. 78)?

Invite participants to explore these difficult questions in pairs. When they have had time to work, invite them to share insights from their conversations, focusing on the ways we face current choices and challenges.

Closing Prayer

God of righteousness, you promise comfort and consolation to all who answer your call to faithful obedience. Help us to use the powerful gift of free will in ways that honor you and bring justice to our world. We are your church, your witness in and for the world; and so we pray in the name of Jesus the Christ. Amen.

NEXT SESSION

Invite participants to

- read chapters 7–8 in the study book and Revelation 8:6–14:5 in advance of the next session;
- reflect on and journal about the beatitudes listed at the end of Session 1. Ask them to consider one insight they might want to share with the group about the second beatitude, Revelation 14:13.

Session 4
THE DRAGON, THE BEASTS, AND SEVEN TRUMPETS

Covering the following chapters from the study book:

Chapter 7: Sounding the Seven Trumpets
Chapter 8: The Satanic Counterfeit: The Dragon
and the Two Beasts
Revelation 8:6–14:5

PLANNING THE SESSION

Session Goals

As a result of conversations and activities connected with this session, group members should begin to

- understand the meaning of *martyrdom*, *elemental* and *demonic forces*, *portent*, and the *number of the beast*;

- reflect on biblical passages related to dragons, God's call, and metaphoric visions;
- explore the imperial context for Revelation and the woman and the dragon;
- assess our faithfulness as witnesses to God's grace.

Key Verse

> *They have conquered him by the blood of the Lamb*
> *and by the word of their testimony,*
> *for they did not cling to life even in the face of death.*
> *Rejoice then, you heavens*
> *and those who dwell in them!*
>
> (Revelation 12:11-12a)

Special Preparation

- Ask participants to bring their notebooks or electronic journals. Provide writing paper and pens for those who may need them. Have a variety of Bibles available for those who do not bring one.
- Have available a markerboard, large sheets of blank paper or construction paper and colored markers.
- Have available images of imperial Roman coins.
- If group members are not familiar with one another, make nametags available.

Remember that there are more activities than most groups will have time to complete. As leader, you'll want to go over the session in advance and select or adapt the activities you think will work best for your group in the time allotted. Consider your own responses to questions you will pose to the group.

GETTING STARTED

Welcome

As participants arrive, welcome them to the study and invite them to make use of one of the available Bibles, if they did not bring one.

Opening Prayer

Awesome and living God, we are yours. We pray that this time of sharing and learning moves us to more faithful obedience to your call for justice and mercy. In the name of Jesus the Christ, we pray. Amen.

Opening Activities

When all participants have arrived, invite each person to introduce himself or herself by name and to share a memory of the first time he or she read or heard readings from the Book of Revelation. Do not take notes during the introductions.

- Encourage participants to share one new insight from their journals or from the second beatitude, Revelation 14:13.
- The author explores Revelation's rich use of symbols and imagery and their relation to life in the Roman Empire. Ask participants whether this helps them understand the dramatic violence described in the chapters for today's session.

LEARNING TOGETHER

Video Study and Discussion

The Session 4 video explores the importance of Christian witness and the countercultural posture of Christians in the Roman Empire. Play the Session 4 video, titled "The Dragon, the Beasts, and Seven Trumpets," and explore together the following questions:

- What is the importance of Christian witness in our own time? How do Christians bear witness to God and Jesus' lordship today?
- How are you participating in God's commission to the church to bear witness to Christ?
- David deSilva refers to "shrines of human empires" such as temples to the Roman emperor in the cities to which Revelation was addressed. What sites in our own society might be considered similar shrines, though we do not formally worship gods there? (Examples might include sports arenas, televisions, movie theaters.)
- What would it look like for Christians today to witness to the sole lordship of God and Christ in our society? How might we approach public sites or centers of civic pride differently if we side with those who worship the Lamb?

Sources and Comparisons

Metaphoric Visions

Why does John use such vivid imagery in describing the horrors brought about by the blowing of the seven trumpets: demonic locusts, unnatural cavalry? To help answer this question, the author lifts up other biblical examples of metaphoric visions that help readers understand God's purposes. Divide the group in half. Invite one group to read Ezekiel 37 (the valley of the dry bones); invite the other to read Acts 10 (Peter's vision of the sheet with "unclean" food). Ask the groups to write a paraphrase or draw an image of the essence of these visions. What made them helpful to Ezekiel and Peter? to the first readers or hearers of these dramatic stories? to us as the body of Christ?

Plagues

While the ten plagues of Egypt do not directly correspond with the plagues of the seven trumpets in Revelation, it is useful to revisit the Egyptian experience for comparison.

Divide into five small groups. Assign each group one of the chapters from Exodus 7–11. These describe the ten plagues in Egypt before the Exodus. Ask each group to list the plague covered in its assigned chapter and the reason given for the plague. Invite the groups to also review Revelation 8:6–9:21; 11:15-19 and list the plagues wrought at the sounding of the seven trumpets.

When the groups have had time to work, invite them to share their findings and, as they report, post side-by-side lists of the Egyptian plagues and Revelation plagues on markerboard or large paper. What are the differences and similarities between the lists? How do the reasons for the plagues differ?

The Scroll of Prophecy

Ask participants to read, in pairs, Ezekiel 2:8–3:4 and Revelation 10:1-11. Invite them to list the differences and similarities in the call to prophecy for Ezekiel and for John.

Cities of Opposition

The author makes it clear that John was writing about the Roman Empire and the city of Rome, in particular. Invite a volunteer to read Revelation 11:7-8. Then ask for volunteers to read reports of the destruction of Sodom (Genesis 19:12-26) and plagues on Egypt (Exodus 14:1-4, 10-13, 21-29). Ask why the author believes John is comparing Sodom and Egypt to Jerusalem.

Forty-two Months

More new numbers have been introduced in this session's reading. We will examine the number 666 below. Here, we look at the source of the number forty-two months, or three and a half years, 1,260 days (Revelation 11:3; 12:6), and also "a time, and times, and half a time" (Revelation 12:14; see Daniel 12:7). The term "forty-two months" appears twice in our texts (11:2; 13:5). In both instances, it was the time given to evil to exercise authority on earth.

- Share this quotation from the study book:

  > The aggressors have authority only "for forty-two
  > months." This period is also the equivalent of three
  > and a half years and 1,260 days, a term limit that
  > is often assigned to the raging of an oppressor. It is
  > derived from Daniel 9:27 and 12:7, where its primary
  > reference is to the time of defilement of the temple by
  > the "abomination that desolates" set up by Antiochus
  > IV from 167 to 164 BC. (p. 86)

- Invite a volunteer to read the Revelation passages and then
  Daniel 9:27; 12:7.

Breaking the Code

Seven Trumpets

Our author points out that the blowing of the seven trumpets
follows a similar pattern to the opening of the seven seals, with an
interlude between trumpets six and seven.

- Share this quotation from our study book:

  > The judgments that follow each of the first four
  > trumpets are elemental forces of nature, which
  > are directed against the cosmos and which affect
  > humanity indirectly. The last three trumpets call forth
  > demonic forces, falling directly on humanity. (p. 81)

- Divide into two groups. Invite one group to explore the first four
  trumpets (Revelation 8:6-13) and the other group to explore
  the last three trumpets (Revelation 9:1-21; 11:15-19). Have
  them review the sections of the study book related to these
  judgments. Ask them to look for the judgment brought about by
  each trumpet blast, why they believe the author labels it as either
  elemental or *demonic*, and the outcome of the judgment.

- When the groups have had time to work, invite a spokesperson from each group to report on the judgment brought on by each trumpet blast and insights gained from the study book and the group conversation.

Interlude: The Scroll and Two Witnesses

Invite participants to review Revelation 10:1–11:14. After they have had time to read, lead a conversation on the reason for this interlude between the sixth and seventh trumpets. If you did not do the earlier exercise, invite a volunteer to read Ezekiel 2:8–3:4 and compare the scrolls described there and in Revelation 10:1-11. Why is John called to measure only certain portions of the temple? What happens to the two witnesses?

The Woman and the Dragon

Invite volunteers to read Revelation 12:1-17. Have the group follow along and read together aloud verses 10b-12. Ask participants to share what they learned about this passage from the study book (see pp. 91–94): Who is the woman? Who is the dragon? Who is the child? What does the word *portent* mean? How does the author define *martyrdom*? Is death necessary for one to be a martyr?

The Counterfeit Trinity

The author describes the dragon of Revelation 12 and the two beasts of Revelation 13 as a "counterfeit trinity" (p. 94): Satan, the Roman emperors, and the false prophet.

- Divide the group in half. Have one group review the related material in the study book and prepare to share its meaning for the first hearers. Have the second group review Revelation 12–13 and prepare to share its meaning for them.
- When the groups have had time to work, invite a spokesperson from each group to share the collective wisdom of the group and compare the learnings from both readings.

Marked for Justice

Again, numbers have great significance in Revelation. In Revelation 14, we see Jesus with the 144,000 martyrs, those who have remained faithful to God, through horrible trials and tortures. They are marked for salvation and redemption, safe from the final judgment.

The famous "number of the beast"—666 (or 616)—is analyzed by the author as referring to the Roman emperor Nero. Those who follow Nero, the powers of this world, are marked on the right hand or the forehead for condemnation.

- Lead a conversation on the differences between these groups.
- If you have images of Roman coins available, include these in your conversation. What is the significance of the coins? (See the author's material on this in the paragraph that begins "One of the ways a ruler…" on pp. 95–96.)
- Be sure to include reference to the author's helpful understanding of the reference to "virgins" in Revelation 14:4.

Practical Revelations

Witnesses

The author suggests that the two witnesses of chapter 11 are not clearly identified so that we might aspire to be such witnesses (see pp. 87–88).

- Invite the participants, in pairs, to discuss this idea. Do they feel they are faithful witnesses to God's righteousness? What would it take for them to become more faithful disciples? What challenges would make it difficult to remain faithful?

Which Power Do We Choose?

Despite all of the horrors inflicted on humanity through the plagues, many of the survivors cling to their sin of idolatry (see p. 83). Even after divine battle and absolute destruction, many choose to be marked by the beast rather than repent and live in faithfulness to God. The author states:

> [M]en and women are so constituted as to worship some absolute power, and if they do not worship the true and real Power behind the universe, they will construct a god for themselves and give allegiance to that. In the last analysis, it is always a choice between the power that operates through domination and inflicting suffering (that is, the power of the beast) and the power that operates through redeeming and restoring, even at the cost of *accepting* suffering (that is, the power of the Lamb). (p. 97)

- Invite a volunteer to read this quotation to the group. Ask if participants agree with this characterization of humanity. Why or why not?

More Perfect Access

The author states: "The issue of all the judgments, the essence of all the rewards, is to have a more perfect access to God and a clearer vision of his splendor" (p. 88).

- Invite participants to respond to this statement in small groups. Why did John feel this was such a central issue for the first hearers? How does the concept of "reward and judgment" align with our understanding of God as Love? Are the rewards of perfect access and clearer vision of God's splendor motivation enough to be faithful in our discipleship? What does that mean?
- When the groups have had time to work, invite a spokesperson from each group to share insights from the collective wisdom shared.

Closing Prayer

God of grace and glory, we have explored, shared, learned, and questioned together. Thank you. Help us to take the lessons from this time into our lives so that people can see your love alive in us. Keep us open to your presence and power. In Christ's name we pray. Amen.

NEXT SESSION

Invite participants to

- read chapters 9–10 in the study book and Revelation 14:6–18:24 in advance of the next session;
- reflect on and journal about the beatitudes listed at the end of Session 1. Ask them to consider one insight they might want to share with the group about the fourth and fifth beatitudes, Revelation 19:9; 20:6.

Session 5
BABYLON AND SEVEN BOWLS

Covering the following chapters from the study book:

Chapter 9: The Seven Bowls of God's Wrath
Chapter 10: Babylon the Great: Toppling Empire and Its Evils
Revelation 14:6–18:24

PLANNING THE SESSION

Session Goals

As a result of conversations and activities connected with this session, group members should begin to

- understand the meaning of *Imperial Rome, Armageddon, "eternal" damnation*;
- reflect on biblical passages related to the seven bowls of God's wrath and the fall of Babylon/Rome;

- explore the injustices that lead to judgment and the power of language;
- assess our choices in faithful living.

Key Verse

Here is a call for the endurance of the saints, those who keep the commandments of God and hold fast to the faith of Jesus.

And I heard a voice from heaven saying, "Write this: Blessed are the dead who from now on die in the Lord." "Yes," says the Spirit, "they will rest from their labors, for their deeds follow them."

(Revelation 14:12-13)

Special Preparation

- Ask participants to bring their notebooks or electronic journals. Provide writing paper and pens for those who may need them. Have a variety of Bibles available for those who do not bring one.
- Have available a markerboard, large sheets of blank paper or construction paper and colored markers
- Have available images of artists' renderings of Armageddon.
- If group members are not familiar with one another, make nametags available.

Remember that there are more activities than most groups will have time to complete. As leader, you'll want to go over the session in advance and select or adapt the activities you think will work best for your group in the time allotted. Consider your own responses to questions you will pose to the group.

GETTING STARTED

Welcome

As participants arrive, welcome them to the study and invite them to make use of one of the available Bibles, if they did not bring one.

Opening Prayer

Great and glorious God, we struggle with the power of these words from your Holy Book. Help us to find together understanding, insight, wisdom, and grace. In the name of Christ we pray. Amen.

Opening Activities

When all participants have arrived, invite each person to introduce himself or herself by name and to share one lasting image from this week's reading. Do not take notes during the introductions.

- Encourage participants to share one new insight from their journals and from the fourth and fifth beatitudes (Revelation 19:9; 20:6).
- Share the images of Armageddon you have available. Ask participants how these compare with their mental images of the final devastation of earth by heavenly forces.
- The author states: "Revelation 14:6-20 is perhaps the clearest portion of the book" (p. 99). Invite volunteers to read these verses and ask if the participants agree that they provide clarity. Why or why not?

LEARNING TOGETHER

Video Study and Discussion

The Session 5 video explores John's harsh critique of Roman imperialism and how we might apply the same perspective in our present day. Play the Session 5 video, titled "Babylon and Seven Bowls," and explore together the following questions:

- What is one thing you learned in the video that you did not know before?
- Given the discussion in the video, what opportunities and challenges do you see in our day-to-day lives for living in a way that would meet with God's approval?

- John's portrayal of Rome called attention to the suffering within the empire that Roman propaganda often hid. What hidden suffering exists in our world today, and how might we hold it up to the light to see things as they really are?
- How do the values of the kingdom of God run counter to the values of our lives today? What challenges does this pose for wholehearted discipleship? How can Scripture reinforce God's values in our lives?

Sources and Comparisons

Great Wine Press of the Wrath of God

John draws on dramatic images from Isaiah to describe the reaping of the earth.

- Divide into two groups. Have one group read Isaiah 63:1-6; have the other read Revelation 14:14-20.
- Invite each group to discuss their responses to these passages and why they believe the authors of Isaiah and Revelation chose such bloody images.
- When the groups have had time to work, invite a spokesperson from each group to share the responses.

Songs of Divine Victory

The author compares the Song of the Lamb in Revelation 15:3-4 with the song of Moses in Exodus 15:1-18 (see pp. 102–104) and other Old Testament passages.

- Invite volunteers to read each of these passages. As they read, have the rest of the participants note similarities and differences.
- Divide into small groups or pairs. Invite each small group or pair to explore the song of the Lamb and compare it with one of the verses listed below, noting similarities in language and message.

Psalm 111:2	Great are the works of the Lord, / studied by all who delight in them.
Psalm 139:4	Even before a word is on my tongue, / O Lord, you know it completely.
Deuteronomy 32:4	The Rock, his work is perfect, / and all his ways are just. / A faithful God, without deceit, / just and upright is he.
Psalm 145:17	The Lord is just in all his ways, / and kind in all his doings.
Jeremiah 10:7	Who would not fear you, O King of the nations? / For that is your due; / among all the wise ones of the nations / and in all their kingdoms / there is no one like you.
Psalm 96:9	Worship the Lord in holy splendor; / tremble before him, all the earth.

- When the groups have had time to work, ask the participants why they believe John drew so heavily from the Hebrew Scriptures. What would have been the impact on the first hearers?

Armageddon

If you did not share images of the battle of Armageddon during the opening activities, you might want to do so now. Read Revelation 16:12-16 as you share the images.

Invite volunteers to read the second to last paragraph of chapter 9 in the study book, where the author shares information about the meaning of the word *Armageddon* (*Harmagedon* in the NRSV). It can also be helpful to explore the context of battles related to Megiddo. Be sure to note that this is not the focus of Revelation, but simply the site of one of the final plagues.

- Divide into three groups. Assign each group one of the passages referenced in the study book: Judges 5:19-21 (from the Song of Deborah); 2 Kings 9:27 (killing of King Ahaziah of Judah); 2 Kings 23:29 (death of the good king, Josiah). Ask them to also read the surrounding text and prepare to share the story or context for the events that occur in Megiddo in each case.
- When the groups have had time to work, invite them to share the stories with the group.

Rome as Babylon

At the beginning of chapter 10 in the study book, the author makes it clear that John is writing about Rome, although Babylon is the name used for the doomed city/empire. It will be helpful to explore some of the sources with which John's audience would be familiar regarding Babylon.

- Divide into three groups. Assign each group one of the following passages: Psalm 137; Isaiah 13; Jeremiah 51:24-64. Ask the groups to prepare to describe the city to the rest of the group. What is being condemned? What is the nature of the destruction? What is the attitude of the faithful to the city?
- When the groups have had time to work, invite them to share their findings. Ask how John's first hearers might have responded to the mention of Babylon, knowing that it was "code" for the Roman Empire.

Breaking the Code

Seven Bowls

Following the victorious singing by those marked for salvation, the final and decisive series of seven plagues brings to an end the wrath of God (Revelation 16:1-21). The author suggests that John was preparing the church for the suffering to come by the repeated series of judgments (see pp. 105–106): seven seals, seven trumpets, seven thunders (that remain hidden), and now, seven bowls of wrath. Unlike the earlier series, these seven plagues are poured out in rapid succession, with no interlude of positive images to break them up.

- Lead a conversation on new responses to the final seven plagues and on the progression of judgments throughout Revelation. Read, or invite a volunteer to read, the three related paragraphs in the study book: "The author's descriptive details" through "the church must prepare to meet them undaunted" (pp. 105–106).

Rome, the Great Prostitute

In Revelation 17, John paints a horrific picture of Rome, drunk on the blood of the martyrs and seated on a scarlet beast that represents the history of Roman imperialism and oppression. If participants have not read this chapter, invite them to do so now to gain an immediate sense of the graphic power of the language.

The author lists three charges against Rome that John makes through this powerful, symbolic language (p. 114). Divide into three groups and ask each group to explore one of the charges and relate it to the picture John paints of Rome. What is the essence of the sin and why is it so important for Christians to learn about it?

- "it has perpetrated violence upon the peoples of the earth and against any who resisted or, like the Christians, bore witness to a different hope;
- "it has exploited its provinces for its own economic advantage and enjoyment of the lion's share of the world's produce;
- "it has exercised idolatrous arrogance in its claims on its own behalf, that it ruled by the will of the gods and would hold sway forever."

When the groups have had time to work, invite a spokesperson for each group to share their learnings.

Fall of Rome

Revelation 18 is a funeral dirge for Babylon/Rome. It may be that the most effective means of understanding its power is to read it. Invite volunteers to provide the various voices and to practice their readings before sharing them aloud. Assign the verses as follows:

- *Narrator:* 1-2a, 4a, 9-10a, 11-13, 15, 17b-18a, 19a, 20-21a
- *Voice A:* 2b-3
- *Voice B:* 4b-8
- *Voices C & D:* 10b
- *Voices E & F:* 14, 16-17a

- *Voices G & H:* 18b, 19b
- *Voice I:* 21b-24

Practical Revelations

Why Choose God?

The author suggests that there are two reasons to choose God rather than the forces of earthly power: (1) "as Creator and Sustainer of all that is, God alone merits worship and ultimate allegiance (see [Revelation] 4:11)"; (2) "because God will hold all creation accountable to God's commandments, this is the only advantageous course of action in the long run!" (p. 100).

- Lead a conversation on participant responses to these reasons for choosing God. Do participants agree with these reasons? Why or why not? How do they align with the reasons participants choose to be Christians? What are other reasons for choosing God?

Free Will and Eternal Damnation

There is a dramatic finality to the judgments of Revelation. How does this align with our understanding of free will and the God of love? Share with the group, this quotation from the study book:

> God respects our free will and will never force us to turn to him. So [these pictures] of wrath and hell [mean] nothing more or less than the terrible truth that the sufferings of those who persist in rejecting God's love in Christ are self-imposed and self-perpetuated. The inevitable consequence is that if they persist in such rejection, God will never violate their personality. Whether any soul will in fact eternally resist God, we cannot say. (p. 101)

- Invite participants, in pairs, to share their responses to this statement about free will and their opinion or feelings about the idea of eternal damnation. How do these ideas impact their day-to-day relationship with God and with others?

- When the pairs have had time to share with each other, invite them to share with the larger group, if they wish to do so.

Systemic Injustice

Share with the group the author's suggestion that the voice from heaven: "Come out of her, my people, so that you do not take part in her sins, and so that you do not share in her plagues" (18:4) is calling us, as well, to awareness of our complicity in systemic injustice: "one [cannot] enjoy the profits of an unjust system without also sharing in the guilt of that unjust system" (p. 114).

- Invite volunteers to read the last two paragraphs of chapter 10 in the study book.
- Lead a conversation on the relevance of these warnings in our time. What are our idols? Where is there injustice in our society and culture? In what ways are we participating in injustice by enjoying its benefits?
- What can we do to address these issues?

Closing Prayer

Creator and sustainer of all that is, we freely choose faithful obedience to your loving will. Help us to see and to work to address injustice in our communities and our world. In Christ's name we pray. Amen.

NEXT SESSION

Invite participants to

- read chapters 11–12 in the study book and Revelation 19:1–22:21 in advance of the next session;
- reflect on and journal about the beatitudes listed at the end of Session 1. Ask them to consider one insight they might want to share with the group about the sixth and seventh beatitudes, Revelation 22:7, 14.

Session 6
NEW HEAVEN AND NEW EARTH

Covering the following chapters from the study book:

Chapter 11: The Final Victory and the Last Judgment
Chapter 12: John's Vision of the Heavenly Jerusalem
Revelation 19:1–22:21

PLANNING THE SESSION

Session Goals

As a result of conversations and activities connected with this session, group members should begin to

- understand the meaning of *millennium, second death, Alpha and Omega*;
- reflect on biblical passages related to Last Judgment, New Heavens and New Earth;

- explore lessons learned about the Book of Revelation;
- assess the impact on their discipleship from this study of the Book of Revelation.

Key Verse

> *The Spirit and the bride say, "Come."*
> *And let everyone who hears say, "Come."*
> *And let everyone who is thirsty come.*
> *Let anyone who wishes take the water of life as a gift.*
>
> *(Revelation 22:17)*

Special Preparation

- Ask participants to bring their notebooks or electronic journals. Provide writing paper and pens for those who may need them. Have a variety of Bibles available for those who do not bring one.
- Have available a markerboard, large sheets of blank paper or construction paper and colored markers.
- If group members are not familiar with one another, make nametags available.

Remember that there are more activities than most groups will have time to complete. As leader, you'll want to go over the session in advance and select or adapt the activities you think will work best for your group in the time allotted. Consider your own responses to questions you will pose to the group.

GETTING STARTED

Welcome

As participants arrive, welcome them to the study and invite them to make use of one of the available Bibles, if they did not bring one.

Opening Prayer

Lord Jesus, Alpha and Omega, with all the host of heaven, we sing Hallelujah! Guide our sharing in this time and our lives in this world. We live in the hope of your new heaven and new earth. Amen.

Opening Activities

When all participants have arrived, invite each person to introduce himself or herself by name and to share a favorite image or verse from the Book of Revelation. Do not take notes during the introductions.

- Encourage participants to share one new insight from their journals or from their understanding of the sixth and seventh beatitudes, Revelation 22:7, 14.
- Each session's preparation has included focus on one or more of the seven beatitudes in Revelation, which we introduced in Session 1. Invite participants to share, in pairs, which of the beatitudes resonates most clearly for them, and why. What has changed in their understanding of these blessings through the course of the study?

LEARNING TOGETHER

Video Study and Discussion

The Session 6 video explores John's vision of judgment and the ultimate arrival of the new Jerusalem, with its promises of justice and hope. Play the Session 6 video, titled "New Heaven and New Earth," and explore together the following questions:

- In what way do John's visions of judgment call us to self-examination? How closely do our lives and practices align with the victims or the perpetrators of injustice?
- How does Revelation point to the importance not only of believing but also of living as those who have believed? What is the difference?

- To what extent do our actions bear witness that we have truly committed ourselves to Jesus Christ in trust and faithfulness?
- How are we making room in our lives, and in our life together, for God's peace and wholeness to break into our world?
- How can we live in a way that points to the reality of God's kingdom right now?

Sources and Comparisons

The Bride and the Lamb

Revelation is filled with glorious images of heavenly worship, in the symbolic language of John. Read 19:1-10, and have all participants read aloud the words of worship in these verses.

We have explored much of this imagery in previous sessions. Here, it will be helpful to look more closely at the sources for the imagery of the city of Jerusalem (or the faithful community) as a bride. The idea of the faithful community as a bride may seem sexist to our modern ears, but it is important to understand the context of this image and how beautiful and inspiring it would be for the first hearers.

- Divide into three groups. Assign one of the following passages to each group and ask them to prepare a description or picture of the bride found there: Isaiah 62:1-5; Ezekiel 16:1-14; Hosea 2:16-20. Let them know that they will have to use their "disciplined imaginations" in creating their images.
- When the groups have had time to work, invite a spokesperson from each group to share their description or picture. Ask if the study of Revelation made it easier to build an image from the symbolic language of the passages. In what ways?

Gog and Magog

The beast, the false prophet, and the dragon—the "counterfeit trinity"—are defeated (19:17–20:3). At the end of a thousand years, Satan is released and attacks the "beloved city" with Gog and Magog. Invite volunteers to read aloud Ezekiel 38, each taking a paragraph, and then Revelation 20:7-10. Ask participants to share in pairs why they think John used "Gog and Magog" as Satan's allies in the final attack.

New Heavens and New Earth

John describes the New Jerusalem as a bejeweled, glittering city, filled with God's light of glory. This may or may not be an appealing image to participants. It will be helpful to explore some of the other descriptions of heaven, or heavenly perfection, found in the Bible.

- Divide into five small groups or pairs. Assign each group Revelation 21:9–22:5 and one of the following texts: Genesis 2:4b-25; Exodus 3:7-8; Isaiah 65:17-25; 2 Corinthians 3:17-18; 5:1-10, 16-17; Colossians 3:1-4.
- Ask each group to create an image of John's vision of the New Jerusalem and a description or image from the alternative, assigned text.
- When the groups have had time to work, invite a spokesperson from each group to share their images/descriptions.
- Lead a conversation on which of the images of perfection resonates most strongly with the participants. Why is one more appealing than another? What changes when we picture heaven or God's kingdom as a way of being rather than a physical space? Ask the group to respond to the idea that the New Jerusalem is to creation as Jesus is to God's people.

Breaking the Code

Seven Visions

Revelation is a book of visions. The phrase, "I saw..." occurs thirty-five times in the text. It's interesting that the author focuses on the rapid succession of seven visions that prepare us for the final victory and judgment: Revelation 19:11, 17, 19; 20:1, 4, 11, 12 (see p. 119).

- Divide into seven pairs. Assign one of the "I saw" texts to each pair (or individual). Invite them to explore the vision, using

NEW HEAVEN AND NEW EARTH

the study book and related Scripture references, and prepare to share the assigned vision (in images, story, song, or summary).

- When the pairs have had time to work, tell the story of the final heavenly victory and the Last Judgment, with each pair presenting in turn.

Book of Merit; Book of Mercy

In exploring the Last Judgment (Revelation 20:11-15), the author speaks of the Book of Merit and the Book of Mercy (book of life).

- Divide the group in half. Assign one of these books to each group and ask them to explore the study book and related Scripture references to describe the book and explain its significance in the Last Judgment (see pp. 124–126).
- When the groups have had time to work, invite a spokesperson from each group to share their collective wisdom.

New Jerusalem and Jesus

At the beginning of chapter 12, the author speaks of the new Jerusalem as either a new creation or a total transformation of the Creation. In what ways does this relate to the impact of the Incarnation in our lives? Ask the group to respond to the idea that the New Jerusalem is to Creation as Jesus is to God's people.

Practical Revelations

Small and Great

Invite a volunteer to read Revelation 19:5. The author states: "This comprehensive phrase, 'small and great,' includes believers of all classes and abilities, and of all stages of progress in their Christian life" (p. 118).

- Lead a conversation about this statement. What does the author mean? Ask participants if they agree or disagree and why. What is the significance of this statement for our personal and corporate discipleship?

Millennialism

The author offers descriptions of three schools of interpretation regarding the millennium. Our view of the end times has profound influence on our values and behavior now.

- Divide into three groups, and ask each group to prepare an argument for one of the three positions: postmillennialists, premillennialists, amillennialists.
- When the groups have had time to work, invite a spokesperson from each group to share and provide evidence for their position.
- When all three groups have presented, invite participants to share which position resonates most deeply for them, and why. Ask them to share how their view influences their lives now.

And Finally, Encouragement and Hope

Invite a volunteer to read the final paragraph of the study book (p. 136). Lead a conversation about lessons learned through the study:

- Where have participants found encouragement and hope in the Book of Revelation? What has been challenging?
- What has changed in their relationship with God, with themselves, with others as a result of this study?

Closing Prayer

Gracious and glorious God, we have explored, shared, learned, and questioned together. Thank you. Help us to take the lessons from this time into our lives so that people can see your love alive in us. Keep us open to your presence and power.

Amen. Come, Lord Jesus!

The grace of the Lord Jesus be with all the saints. Amen.

(Revelation 22:20b-21)